THE JOY OF HEAVEN 4

Onward They Flew

Advantage
BOOKS
www.advbookstore.com

Written and Illustrated by
Daniel Leske

"…they shall MOUNT up with wings as eagles…" Isaiah 40:31

I0098161

The Joy of Heaven 4: Onward They Flew by Daniel Leske
Copyright © 2016 by Daniel Leske
All Rights Reserved.
ISBN: 978-1-59755-408-4

Published by: ADVANTAGE BOOKS™
Longwood, Florida, USA
www.advbookstore.com

This book and parts thereof may not be reproduced in any form, stored in a retrieval system or transmitted in any form by any means (electronic, mechanical, photocopy, recording or otherwise) without prior written permission of the author, except as provided by United States of America copyright law.

Library of Congress Catalog Number: 2016916054

First Printing: November 2016
16 17 18 19 20 21 22   10 9 8 7 6 5 4 3 2 1
Printed in the United States of America

FROM THE AUTHOR

As the author, I thought that there would only be three books in this series, yet with inspired writing, one doesn't know the total will of the Lord. He opened the door again so this story could continue with more on the inside of heaven.

This happens as I walk and do things, yet pretty soon I am thinking the Lord wants me to do more writing for him. Then it may be days or weeks and the feeling gets stronger until the pressure becomes very strong to one. At that time, I realize the Lord is wanting my attention, so the next step is to plan time to find out if the writing is there.

These books have been written between 2 am and 5am in the morning. I simply get out plenty of paper with pen and within hours of the writing the scene starts to unfold of where chapter one begins for each book. From there I just write, sometimes trying hard to keep up with the speed of words coming forth. In my spirit, I feel like I am always about 5 to 10 feet away from Wee Angel and Felicia as the story proceeds!

Whether writing or painting on a religious artwork, many times I have felt the Holy Spirit take hold of the pen or brush with his strength to see it gets done right. It is a gift! The experience of some of the events in this book, I cannot easily get over and I believe it's meant to be that way! INSPIRED WRITING!

I realized that how we approach the Lord on earth prepares us for what he wants of us in heaven. An example is if you pray and praise him here, then you will fit into the praise and prayer services in heaven. We are being molded here. Also it is never to late to know the Lord or to do something for Him.

Hopefully these books will help you, open doors in your life, and that's what I pray as the author for you.

Our Creator is Special. He made earth that way! He made heaven that way! As the Lord said that He is the WAY! The Holy Spirit is the guide!

The journey continues with Wee Angel and Felicia meeting more friends and seeing the beauty of heaven. Maybe as you read, He will show you a quick glimpse of heaven. Enjoy book 4 and book 5 will be coming in time. God bless!

A friend,

DANIEL

List of Characters

Wee Angel:	She has white hair and is always a little smaller than any of the other angels.
Felicia:	She is about 8 or 9 years old in stature with blonde hair.
Angel Gabriella:	The identical twin of Angel Daniella.
Angel Daniella:	The identical twin of Angel Gabriella.
Sir William (Revelation):	A very SPECIAL white winged horse.
Annie:	A tall cougar with wings.
Tuddley Teddy:	A brown bear that is a friend to everyone.
Lord God Almighty:	He rules heaven and earth from his throne in heaven.
Angel Angelina:	Angel guide to mansions.
Angel Hannah:	Angel guide to mansions.
Jesus:	Commander-in-Chief of the heavenly army.
David and Joshua:	From the Bible: Leaders of the riders on white winged horses.
Noah:	A awesome winged lion.
Majestic:	A blue heron that is always with Noah.
Angel Jennifer:	Angel guide to mansions.
Golden:	A white winged leopard.
Starbright:	A brown winged horse with glowing star and white socks.
Zechariah:	A moose with antlers that glisten!

Daniel Leske

ARCHANGELS

Michael, Micah, Gabriel   The Lord's power angels.
and Raphael:

Also thousands and Thousands of angels, others from Bible that are also leaders of the riders, saints, and other friends.

The Lord decided to open the door more! The inspired writing continues in book 4, *"ONWARD THEY FLEW."* Wee Angel and Felicia continue to visit more prayer areas and more about God's Holy City. An awesome thought, Felicia said, "I'm finally home!" Then they meet Jesus again with David and Joshua from the Bible, including many, many, more white winged horses with power riders. A quiet flight turns into a mission towards EARTH, meeting other formations of these horses with power riders, and led by other names from the Bible. During the flight, the archangels join in! Jesus riding his favorite winged horse, Revelation, is in front and in command. Thousands of angels praising Jesus. Joel 2:30, "And I will show you wonders in the heavens..."

Chapter 1

God's City Gate

Felicia, Wee Angel, Angel Daniella and Angel Gabriella had just finished seeing Lord God Almighty by his throne. They stood along one of the beautiful streets in God's City. Angels flew close by them. Saints walked, praised God and some sang glories to his holy name.

The scene was glorious in God's city. A huge waterfall was far away to their left with the crystal-like waters that slowly came towards them from the distance. These waters came, oh so close, then flowed out and around a huge crystal-like dwelling along the street.

High above them, the angels hovered with instruments, high, up and away! For they were again at another gate ready to leave God's city. This gate again was different from the others. Roses, flowers of many varieties were present. Along it's sides on both sides of the flowered crystal-like gate were golden rays of light streams. There were many small streams with waterfalls that came from high above through glories of light.

They could not see where these streams of water came from above, because the light was so intense that was high above them, with ten to twenty or more streams to each side of this gate.

Flowers were in groups along the streams that flowed away from the gate, and along the golden street.

Several birds including doves flew up and away from a beautiful fruit tree that was close by them.

Wee Angel said to them, "Isn't our Lord wonderful! He again was so kind to us, and gave us hugs."

"What a blessed time we had with him!" added Felicia.

Angel Gabriella said, "Thank you both for taking us with you!"

"Yes, thank you so much!" added Angel Daniella.

Both said to Wee Angel and Felicia that they were going to stay in the city and meet with some other angels.

All gave hugs to each other, said their good days and of course, Wee Angel and Felicia said together, "We will see you again and fellowship!"

Angel Daniella and Angel Gabriella ran back to them and said, "You both are so special! Thank you!"

They stood relishing the moment. The Joy of Heaven was in their hearts.

Their friendship was real and they again talked for quite awhile about everything which led to laughing and even crying with a few tears.

Felicia said, "I've seen so much since I've been in heaven."

Quietly, Angel Gabriella and Angel Daniella flew above the golden street back into the city of God's.

Wee Angel and Felicia strolled along the street whistling, just as Felicia and her had whistled when she first came to heaven.

Once through the gate of God's City, they paused and prayed together.

Wee Angel said, "Dear Lord, let me continue to show our Felicia more of heaven and what you have created here."

Felicia said, "Thank you again Lord for everything that I've seen and looked at, and been apart of here. We love you so much! Thank you! Amen!"

As they finished their prayer an angel flew up beside them. She greeted them. Wee Angel knew her and said her name was Angel Hannah. She said that the Lord wanted her to guide, be with them and to see more of heaven. They talked and had fellowship for a short time. Angel Hannah had on a very beautiful light blue gown with golden rings on the collar. There were golden rings on the sleeves. Her hair was white like Wee Angel's hair. She had the biggest smile and her eyes sparkled of radiant light. All the eyes of the angels had light that flowed from them, yet it was so soft! Felicia was so awed by them and continued to be so since she had arrived into heaven.

With that, they started to fly along the golden road further away from God's City. Glories of light were all around with such awesome light! The gate glowed with this light as they looked back at it, with vines going upward along its sides, as there were more streams, and more flowers! It was like a crystal-like mountain with falls on the inside of the gate, and outside of the gate were vines on the mountainsides.

Chapter 2

Walkways

They flew over and along the hills. Glories filled the heavenly skies about them, as they passed over flowered groupings, and forest groupings of trees.

Some of the trees had special glowing colors, streaming from their peaks. Radiant streams of light flowed from the peaks of the trees.

Then in the distance were more bluish mountains and above them special streams of light that went horizontal with the mountains.

"Felicia, they are glory streams that in some areas go just above heaven's lands. We are going to go and fly in them to another special place in heaven." said Angel Hannah.

Onward they flew towards these glory lights.

Once there, they flew into the bright stream of light that was flowing in heaven's skies above these mountains.

Onward! Onward, they flew in this light stream.

Felicia said, "My! Wee Angel, this is so wonderful. It's like this is carrying us as well as our flying in it."

They could see a little of heaven's lands flashing below them as they were traveling at very high speeds to another part of heaven. Everything passed very quickly to their heavenly eyes.

On and on and on, they flew with the light all around them. Soon they were flying away from heaven's lands, but still in the light stream. Within heaven's time Angel Hannah said, "We are going to fly out of the stream."

So they did! Just as they flew out they were in a region of heaven that had beautiful celestial walkways that were all around them.

"Wee Angel, it's like walkways in clouds with straight walkways between them." Felicia said as she looked about at the surroundings.

They flew into a courtyard of glowing lights with tables, flowing waters, flowers and stones that glowed! One could look through them, as they were celestial stones. This courtyard was like a balcony that overlooked the valley.

Angels and some saints with wings were present there.

Felicia pointed as she said, "Look all around us to the horizon. As far as we can see, clouds, valleys formed by clouds. Glories of light are all around us. Below us! Above us! It's beautiful, Wee Angel! Oh my!"

There was no bottom or top. They were in the celestial with clouds and walkways, places to visit, areas to praise the Lord, to fellowship with others. Hallelujah's seemed to fill the heavenly, celestial skies. They could see many of these balcony-like courtyards amongst the valley of clouds as they looked over the region.

Angel Hannah said, "Remember many of the angels are always in the glories of light. For many it is their way of life and that is what God created them for as He is Spirit."

They heard the sounds of angels with instruments. There was a tremendous feeling of rejoicing as they looked at everything.

As far as Angel Hannah, Felicia and Wee Angel could see were the celestial cloud-like clouds with many angels and saints. Many angels flew about as well! "It feels so differently when you can't see any of heaven's lands." said Felicia.

"Your alright, though, Felicia." comforted Wee Angel to Felicia. "Heaven is vast and celestial too! The Joy of Heaven is real, Felicia. Just know that!"

Chapter 3

Noah and Majestic

Wee Angel and Felicia were amazed and awed at their surroundings. Here it was just different then the places they had been before with it's openness and vastness in all directions.

Yet, they felt God's awesomeness as always!

Wee Angel said, "Felicia, this is another place in heaven and there are many like this!"

They rested by some fountains of water, which were apart of this celestial place. The colors were of the most beautiful blues to the open spaces above and to the sides of everything.

"Look upwards, Wee Angel." said Felicia.

The openness with cloud-like forms spiraled up and away as high as they could look above them.

In this spiral of heavenly space they saw angels hovering and singing in the light cloud-like stairways that seemingly floated about them.

"Felicia, just like we said of the angels above, that's what we now are apart of here." said Wee Angel. Angel Hannah listened to Wee Angel and Felicia as they talked about everything.

They stood on the cloud-like stairs, yet they had and could see far away! They could fly to other places, about and around them where they could rest such as a courtyard and dwelling places. Crystal-like dwelling places with bright lights were all about them.

Angels, saints, special prayer areas and special celestial falls of water and light that cascaded ever so slowly to the next lower level.

Each area was in a cloud-like light, yet the most beautiful blues of heaven were in all directions.

There were areas where there were many stairways, yet still angels and saints with wings could fly from one place to another.

"This is so beautiful!" said Felicia. "I am sure understanding more about the angels, their wings and why wings are so special!"

Wee Angel said, "Let's pray! Thank you God for Felicia, Angel Hannah, and our journey. Thank you that we could come here to visit other angels and saints." "Thank you Lord," added Felicia. "We love you!"

At that time Angel Samuel came and talked with them. Then came Angel Benjamin, Angel Ritah, Angel Angella, Angel Hebron, Angel Isaac, Angel Sarah, and Angel Pauline!

Now with them came a beautiful winged lion and on his back was a large blue heron. Angel Hannah said the lion's name was Noah and the blue heron's name was Majestic. Noah, right away, liked Felicia and Wee Angel. He was not a overly big lion, just a nice lion. He seemed so much like Tuddley Teddy in his ways. He also liked attention so he made sure that Wee angel and Felicia knew this by putting his head right close to them. Majestic was like his name as he was large, beautiful and always liked to be around Noah.

"Oh Noah is so cuddly!" said Felicia as she rubbed him up by his ears. Wee Angel had already found a nice place on his back.

Both enjoyed him. Felicia was now getting used to the animals with wings while Angel Hannah smiled as she put her hands on Noah's back. Majestic was in flight, as he decided to circle around everyone, but soon landed, walked up to Wee Angel and Felicia for their attention.

Within heaven's time Angel Hannah said to Felicia and Wee Angel, "We are going to be going back to heaven's lands."

They gave hugs to each one and soon they flew upwards towards another stream of light and into it. Then, just behind Angel Hannah, Felicia and Wee Angel flew Noah the winged lion and Majestic, as they were determined to follow them.

Onward and onward, they flew in the light.

Felicia said to Wee Angel, "Where we just came from is so different, yet the glories and holiness of God are so strong there!"

Onward they flew and soon they landed back on heaven's lands.

Chapter 4

Heaven is My Home

Angel Hannah, Wee Angel, Felicia, Noah and Majestic landed back on heaven's lands with its rolling hills, flowers, golden roads and beautiful waters. They were still in total awe with what they had seen in the celestial dwelling place. Angel Hannah said that another angel guide would be joining them. She said her good-days to Felicia and Wee Angel. They had hugs and many smiles, and Noah made sure he got his share. Soon Angel Hannah was gone and in flight to another place to guide others!

"Felicia," Wee Angel said, "God said, I was to continue to take you to many places in heaven for a time yet!"

"I am just having so much fun and love in my heart." Felicia added.

Noah was right beside them and within a short distance was a grouping of fruit trees.

"Look at the fruits." spoke up Felicia. "They are so glowing with light."

"They are still edible, so that's what we are going to do, eat some!" Wee Angel said as she gave some attention to Noah and Majestic.

They got some fruit. It was large and round like a grapefruit, yellowish and very glowing of light.

"It tastes like a very sweet lemon." remembered Felicia.

They enjoyed it's wonderful taste.

They sat and Noah came and laid right by them. He placed his head on their laps and he loved to have his head and ears rubbed by them.

"Isn't he beautiful?" said Felicia.

"Yes, he is!" added Wee Angel. "He's nice to have with us."

All rested on God's heaven's grass. They enjoyed the birds that flew past them. They enjoyed the flowers and the their beauties.

Several saints on horses passed on the golden road. Some would stop and dismount, then they had fellowship and shared experiences. There was Jim, Angie, Marcia, Timothy, Andrew, Sarah, and other saints.

They had time for prayer.

Felicia said, "Dear Lord, all of us are so thankful to be a part of your heaven! We love you, Lord! Amen!"

Soon the travelers had left them.

But their company was not over for soon Felicia said, "Look up the golden road. It's Annie and Tuddley Teddy! And they have a moose with them."
Felicia was all smiles.

Wee Angel flew quickly towards them as they were now running! Oh the meeting was so exciting!

After the many hugs, Wee Angel said, "The moose's name is Zechariah."

"I love that! Oh you're so beautiful!" Felicia said. "I love you Zechariah! Annie! Oh how I missed you and Tuddley! I can never get enough of seeing you."

The moment was sweet. Several birds, bluejays, some robins, some cardinals, some song sparrows came by as well! The birds even rested on Noah and Zechariah. They sang with all their might. Wee Angel and Felicia played with the birds as they again would sit and stand for them, as there was no fear in their hearts. There is no fear in heaven. Just is as it is! During this Majestic neatly stood on Zechariah's back.

Annie was so special to them. She came and just in her own cougar way wanted Wee Angel and Felicia to hug her and play with her. She wiggled all over! They were so happy!

Wee Angel and Felicia decided to take some time and be with Tuddley Teddy. He was always so special to them. They spent time combing, as best they could, his fur. He looked at them with his eyes as they spoke so much love in them. They even seemed to water with some tears as they combed and rubbed behind his ears.

Felicia said, "He has been so special for us."

Wee Angel continued, "Felicia, it's heaven's way. You are now apart of this!" Tuddley wiggled now!

They talked, prayed, and played in this beautiful kingdom called Heaven. Their friendship with Tuddley was just a small moment of this.

Wee Angel and Felicia sat while Tuddley laid on the grass with his head on their little laps. He rested, closed his eyes, and enjoyed their attention as he felt so wanted by them. Both looked at his closed eyes and smiled at each other.

Of course, Felicia again had a couple of tears of joy in knowing Wee Angel and Tuddley Teddy. He laid so still as they continued to comb his fur. He lifted his head and looked into their eyes as he showed his gratitude towards them.

Meanwhile Annie and the others laid close by them.

Wee Angel and Felicia reflected again on some moments, such as the praise services, seeing Jesus, the riders, the beautiful winged horses, meeting other saints, angels, the field of lilies, other heavenly animals, birds, and their friends. They sat for quite some time and went over many thoughts and moments!

Then with time, they were rested and ready to see to see more of heaven.

They wanted to spend a little extra time with Tuddley, since he couldn't be with them in their flights. Wee Angel said, "We will be back sometime and spend more time walking with Tuddley."

Soon an angel flew and stood besides them. Wee Angel knew her and said, "Angel Angelina. I'm so blessed to see you again!"

She introduced herself to Felicia and said, "We will be going to another dwelling place or mansion. I'm to take you there!"

So with time, Tuddley Teddy knew he would be on his own again! Zechariah and Tuddley didn't have wings so they would have to stay on heaven's lands. After the good-days and all their hugs, Wee Angel, Felicia, Annie, Noah and Majestic flew in circles around and around, just above Zechariah and Tuddley Teddy.

Tuddley and Zechariah enjoyed the moment, and in fact, they wiggled with heavenly excitement!

Felicia said as they flew, "It's harder to leave Tuddley every time and now Zechariah! He is so beautiful!"

"Felicia, this is heaven. We will see them again and again! Just know that! This is for eternity, Felicia! This is their home and this is your home."

Felicia again showed signs of tears, "My home! My home! Our home! Tuddley's home. Zechariah's home."

They flew over some fields of flowers, more golden roads, streams, and trees on their journey. They had again this joy of heaven in their hearts. They talked more about this home, this home for eternity.

Chapter 5

City of Lights

As they flew along, Felicia smiled and said, "Wee Angel, Oh how Zechariah's antlers glistened, like they were glowing of light, and glistening so strong!" "That's right, Felicia. They are so beautiful!" added Wee Angel.

In the heavenly sky, other saints were on winged horses, angels were in flight, as well as birds, geese, eagles and other birds of heaven.

They flew towards some smaller mountains where vast glories were streaming upwards into the sky.

Soon they were there. They walked on the golden road, as Annie and Noah looked so content and were so happy to be with their friends.

Angel Angelina said, "We are going to take Annie, Majestic, and Noah with us! They can come with us."

Along the golden way were flowers and hedges with beautiful trees in blossom. Soon they walked through the gateway into the light that they would be traveling in to their destination.

Then upward, they flew in this light. They flew! They flew! They flew! They flew in this light. They could see each other, but that was it, for they only saw more light.

These glowing lights were more and more around them. Then finally they flew through another archway and into another dwelling place in heaven.
They landed on the most beautiful golden street, with very silvered edges. They were in another celestial city with it's vast dwellings.

The city was extremely vast!

Wee Angel said to Felicia, "This city is so special! The name of the city is The City of Lights. We are standing in this vast city, yet as we look out and away from here, the small stars make the whole region of this part of the universe look like a beautiful city of lights with the heavens."

"My! Oh My! Oh My!" Felicia kept saying over and over!

It was all lights and very celestial across the regions of this part of heaven as they looked outward away from the city.

They looked around from where they stood by the archway.

It was like a city amongst lights and covered a lot of heavenly space.

They stood on another beautiful golden street with crystal-like dwellings about them, which were upon the sides of the hills of light itself. They glowed with glories of light. Light beams were everywhere as they looked about it.

It was like day, yet it had the vastness of the universe. Stars all about, with no darkness or blackness, but deep blues and hues of very light purples and deep aqua colors to the open heavens around them. There were regions above with clusters of these small lights or star-like areas that glistened and shined through these colors. It was a day scene yet it had the appearance of the universe about it. All around them, up and around at long distances were areas of lights which had dwelling places for those that were there, the saints, and angels.

Noah and Annie stood by Angel Angelina and were so content to be with their friends. Felicia and Wee Angel continued to look at everything about and around them.

The hills around them had soft glowing lights. The dwelling places or mansion-like homes were the most beautiful golden tones with crystal-like hues of light radiating around them.

Angel Angelina said to them, "We are going to now fly to some places here."

With that Wee Angel, Felicia, and Angel Angelina stood and prayed and thanked the Lord for everything. So much to see and the beauty of it.

Chapter 6

The City is Vast

There were also streams of water, which flowed over small waterfalls between the dwelling places. There were pearl-like walls that had gems of radiant light coming from them. The streams flowed along the golden street.

They saw valleys of lighted dwellings to one side and also other hills, as they were more on the topside of the city.

Soon they flew upward above the hills and dwellings into more golden light. As they flew upward they saw how the city went as far as their heavenly eyes could see amongst the gentle radiant hills of lights that went upwards and then there were more areas of hills. There were hundreds of little waterfalls and streams that went amongst the dwellings.

Angels and Saints flew everywhere! As they looked again, above and around, they saw groupings of smaller light-like stars so this area of heaven was amongst the stars and made up the City of Lights. It was so vast!

They landed next to some more dwelling places, again with falls of water and light. They then walked and flew to a beautiful prayer sanctuary where the sides were beams of light, high falls of light that slowly streamed to the heavenly land.

Thousands of angels were there in praise, and some saints were present there. Three angels came up to visit with them, and again just a little taller than Wee Angel. They talked, and they gave Noah, Majestic and Annie some attention too as they stood by a large waterfall. It had vines along the sides with flowers that glowed like light. The fragrance of the flowers was awesome!

High above to one of the sides was another region of the city with it's glowing lights. It was again above and away from them. High above with beams of light and glories of light around it as if in a cloud-like mansion. Between this area of dwelling places, were some pinnacles with streams of water flowing, many, many steps of water flowed from high, to sides and along the street, from the cloud-like mansions down to the street.

Fires of light, soft fires of light hovered in the heavenly sky.

"Look," Felicia said, "Nothing is holding in these fires of light above and to the sides. They are everywhere, even out and away from the city."

The crystal-like waters flowed over steps of golden glass-like hills and ridges. The waters cascaded from above to lower depths. All flowed into a large stream or river, and then flowed along the golden street.

Angels and saints walked past them. Some would stop and play with Noah and Annie, while Felicia was so awed to be there. It wasn't too long and along side of two angels walked a white leopard, very white with light golden spots.

Felicia introduced herself, "This is Wee Angel and I am Felicia. What's the beautiful leopard's name?"

Angel Hebron said, "Golden."

"Oh that's beautiful!" said Felicia.

Wee Angel said, "He is very special!"

Angel Hebron said, "Golden is to go with you for awhile. We were told to bring him to you."

"Again he has wings too!" said Felicia, realizing the wings were much more a part of the heavenly life.

They prayed and thanked the Lord. It was always a part of meeting others to be thankful.

Above the city, were glowing lights that glowed softly, very softly, yet they saw the deep blues.

There are different regions; they are out and away from the earth. Lord God said in his Word, Psalms 147: 8, "Who covereth the heaven with clouds... ."

These are the clouds in the universe and can be the clouds around earth, yet people on earth cannot see heaven because of this.

All of them hugged and soon they were ready to leave.

Angel Angelina picked a couple of orchid flowers that were close by, and put them in the coats of the three winged friends.

There were celestial bushes of orchids, roses, daffodils, irises, and some very glowing type celestial trees by them. Light flowed right through them and light came out of them. Silver type places they could sit were there.

The dwellings or mansions were awesome that they saw along the river and by the waterfalls. There were mansions between waterfalls and streams. Some dwelling places looked like they were set into the glowing hills such that the waters flowed right over the top of them, across the mansion to another stream, yet the mansion or dwelling place was never overly done. Always in the beauty of the surroundings like the falls, not too ornate or gaudy, just the tiniest gems, beautiful golds, silvers with wood-like blending in some like the cedar woods.

"What beautiful sounds and music, we hear!" Wee Angel said, "Felicia, Angel Angelina, there are many vast beautiful prayer areas, sanctuaries, and praise services. These are all apart of his glories."

At times groups of angels flew past them and at times beautiful heavenly sounds filled the heavenly skies.

There was no darkness, the outer skies were again, blues, and glow-like so that everything was of light and no darkness like nights on earth.

Balcony-like areas, outdoor areas like a beautiful patio setting with shrubs, waterfalls, waters, and with light or of light. Beautifully done by the Creator.

Chapter 7

Light beams
and
Glories with Praise

They went to another beautiful archway, and soon were in flight to another beautiful place. In heaven's time they came through an archway that was all vines with flowers. Amongst the vines were thousands of little light beams. Gems made up the base with walls of gems around it.

Up in the cloud-like sky, far away, were areas of many glories of light.

Angel Angelina said, "In the strong glories of light are more areas with dwellings or mansions, patio areas like here."

Then Angelina said, "We are going to another special mansion in the City of Lights."

They found another beautiful archway with light. Soon they were in flight to another place of this City of Lights. They flew through another gate and then looked high above them. The heavenly sky was formed like a huge dome of clouds that formed the walls to this celestial area.

There were lights all about, in the clouds with small glowing fires of light. Beautiful golden, yellow tones that went far out and away from where they stood on the most beautiful golden area.

To their sides, were a couple of high waterfalls with golden colored trees close to a river of golden waters which went away from the falls that came from high above in the cloud-like sky. They were in a valley, with the edges of the mountains close by them.

Upon the mountains were more areas of golden lights, with beautiful mansion-like dwellings, making up a city. Lights beamed from these dwellings. Beautiful stairways, and golden walkways were all through the mountains. There was so much to see as each one looked about with so much excitement.

They saw many saints and angels. Many were in flight. Glories of light beams going through the high clouds. They heard heavenly praises from the distance, glories to the Father.

Beautiful sounds from the waters.

Everywhere they looked, it was so plush and rich in colors such as the trees, shrubs, and mountains. A beautiful sereneness, yet they heard the awesome sounds of praise. They took time and prayed to the Lord.

Above them on the bluffs were many dwelling, patio-like areas that overlooked the valley. More waterfalls in the distance. Beautiful rainbows above them.

Chapter 8

I'm Home

Soon they decided they should leave and all were up in flight in this light back to where they had started from by God's Holy City.

In the light they flew, Angel Angelina, Wee Angel, Felicia, Noah, Majestic, Golden, and Annie.

They flew! They flew like before a tremendously long distance!

They flew! They flew and finally back to an archway close to where they had left, on the golden path, with some meadows and beautiful lavenders there.

With a forest of tall tees, also hedges of honey-suckle bushes, ponds of glistening waters, with cranes, flamingos, and other heavenly birds close by them.

The scene was serenely beautiful for them especially after all the traveling they had just done in the light.

The animals ran and played together on some of the open grass.

Wee Angel said, "I'll go to some fruit trees and be back with some food for us to enjoy."

Off she went and soon back with food for everyone.

"Angel Angelina, Wee Angel, that was a beautiful, long journey." said Felicia. They ate and then slept in the meadows.

The animals also slept! Majestic found a limb. All were tired from the flight, heavenly tired and they rested a heavenly time. They awoke and praised the Lord! With this Angel Angelina said she had to go, so again good-days were given and the promises that they would again see each other.

"Both of you take care, and I'll see you again!" said Angel Angelina with a little tear in her eye.

Soon she flew off to help at some other place in heaven.

Wee Angel and Felicia talked and reflected on everything. They flew and sat on the backs of their friends who ran and played around the meadows with lavender flowers at it's edges. The golden path was close by them.

Soon, they looked and some saints on horses approached from the forested area. As they drew close, the four saints had another horse with them.

He had wings, was darker brown with four white socks, as people would say who know horses. His mane was very light, and he had a beautiful white shaped star on his forehead that had a glow to it. He was tall and very majestic!

"It's Starbright!" said Wee Angel, "He knows Sir William, as they have flown together many times."

"That's wonderful!" said Felicia.

Starbright saw them and he ran to see them.

Jim, Frank, Ernie, and Joyce got off their horses of different colored browns. They were beautiful tall horses.

The saints visited with both and spent a little time with the animals. They had prayers and said their good-days and left on their beautiful horses.

In heaven's time, two more angels flew from a distance.

Felicia said, "It's Angel Daniella and Angel Gabriella, praise the Lord!"
It was a beautiful sight to see them together again!

"Wee Angel," Felicia said, "This is why heaven is so special! You said to me when I got to heaven that we would see them again and again. Now here are our friends again. The Lord just knows and then it happens. First Starbright came with the saints, now Angel Gabriella and Angel Daniella with this, all in order, that's the way it is here in heaven. I am so glad I am in heaven. This is now my home and I love it so much. I am so happy. Thank you Wee Angel, and thank you Lord. I'm home. I'm finally home!"

Felicia as well as everyone had again the tears of joy in their hearts and some in their eyes.

Felicia had barely finished speaking when Angel Micah soon flew up, greeted them, and then he was gone again.

"That's just what you were saying Felicia, and we have talked about!" added Wee Angel.

Other saints had passed by on the golden paths, with some on horses, and also some angels flew over the meadows.

The scene was heavenly awesome and spoke of the joys and it's heavenly ways. Life in heaven is of beauty, togetherness, fellowship, thankfulness, being considerate, and above all love. It had prayer and through the prayers each became stronger in the heavenly way.

Daniel Leske

Chapter 9

The Prayer Areas
are
Always Beautiful

Along the golden path two little angels, just a little taller than Wee Angel and Felicia, walked towards them. With them was a large lama called Proverbs. Their names were Angel David and Angel Benjamin.

Everyone talked and with time, they prayed, and soon Angel David and Angel Benjamin with Proverbs left on the golden path.

Soon everyone was in flight with Angel Gabriella on the back of Starbright as the rest flew up and above to their next destination in heaven.

In the heavenly skies, they again saw many winged horses with passengers and below them horses on the golden paths. Within heaven's time, they came to another golden gateway of light and glories from which they could fly to another heavenly mansion.

This time they were by several orchards of different fruits with beautiful flowered hedges, smaller hills as well as smaller mountains in the distance and some open waters.

In the same area, was open grass by the fruit trees, so they landed there.

There was a beautiful prayer area amongst these beautiful fruit trees.

Wee Angel said, "All of us, let's take some time for prayer to the Lord."

They decided to leave the winged animals, then walked and enjoyed everything at hand! The four talked, worshiped, talked some more, giggled, laughed and enjoyed this joy of heaven.

They soon came to this large open area amongst apple, orange, apricot, cherry trees and other heavenly fruit trees. Blossoms on many, fruits on many, as they took some time, and had a few fruits as they sat by the trees.

Then in time, they walked into the prayer area where other saints and angels were in prayer.

Special angels hovered around the sides, up and away into the glories of the heavenly sky, just above the prayer area. These grounds were extremely holy as heaven is holy. Always peace with love that filled these heavenly skies.

This time, they spent a lot of time in prayer. They sat, stood, and even laid in prayer. It was glorious, and each knew it's importance. In heaven, it came so easily, it just was and everyone loved it. It was in their heavenly hearts.

As they left, they talked with Angel Anna.

Soon another angel guide flew closer to them. She introduced herself as Angel Jennifer and said to them she would be going with them to the next mansion. Angel Gabriella and Angel Daniella knew her too!

Felicia said, "Your so pretty! Thank you for coming with us."

She was dressed in a gown that sparkled!

A beautiful full gown with bluish type pearls on it and many fine laces.

Within heaven's time, they flew over to the golden gateway. Soon they flew up and away in the golden light as they were being guided by this light. Felicia understood more, this means of travel to other places in heaven.

Onward they flew, until, in front of them they saw their next place to visit in heaven.

Soon they flew out of the light unto a golden path, which had many flowers and shrubs alone the path and a golden gateway with some small streams.

Daniel Leske

Chapter 10

Valley of Prayer

They soon stood in the glories of the gateway and the beauties of this mansion. They were in the most beautiful valley with a mountain range to both sides of the valley.

The whole valley was special prayer and praise grounds. Everything there was for prayer and praise.

"Look at all the angels in the heavenly skies above this valley." said Felicia. "They are all along by the mountains."

"Felicia," Wee Angel said, "In those glories that you see all around and above, angels are hovering!"

Hundreds of small waterfalls in the mountains with some very beautiful flowers. They could see a few of the streams, as these streams flowed out from the mountains and about the whole valley. All of them took some time and went by a stream, off the golden path.

Flowers and beautiful grass were there. Most of the trees were closer to the mountainsides. Saints were there too. They walked about, and praised the Creator for everything. Felicia had tears of joy in her heart, soul and eyes. Then Wee Angel got crying too! Then Angel Daniella got crying too! Then Angel Gabriella got crying! Also Angel Jennifer had tears.

"I'm so happy to be here!" Felicia cried on, "I'm so happy to be here in heaven. Look how beautiful everything is here in heaven. The flowers, waters, and glories above the mountains, angels, are all so beautiful. Again, this is my home!"

The valley was pretty level between the mountain ranges. Above the range were soft glories with beautiful golds, blues, and yellows in colors.

"I'm just so happy!" as Felicia cried more!

Her little heart was so full of joy and so happy with her friends, and animal friends, as well as the time she had already spent with Jesus.

"I'm so happy!" she continued as tears still flowed from her eyes.

Wee Angel said, "This mansion or valley, does this to our heavenly soul and heart. Tears of joy come so easy here. The Creator has made it that way here. It is special for prayer, praise, and thankfulness."

There were short waterfalls and tall waterfalls. There were narrow and wide falls. None were really too wide. Just all very beautiful with vines on their sides. They couldn't see all of them as the valley went out and on, into the glories of light. Close by them were streams with little step waterfalls.

Within heaven's time, Angel Jennifer said they should fly to a few places in the valley.

Up they flew, just above the streams and flowers. They flew over golden paths, streams, flowers, around special prayer and praise areas. They flew past more saints and angels. Then they flew up to the sides of the valley. There they were in an area with some beautiful evergreen trees and they could look out and away into the valley.

There were more falls close by them that flowed ever so slowly over steps, and many turns were in the streams as they slowly made their way to the valley. There were many types of flowers in rows by the sides along the stream's edges.

There was another archway that was along the mountainside.

Felicia said, "Oh the peace and love here. Everything is so quietly awesome!"

The archway was a distance from them, yet they saw beautiful vines with flowers going up and along it's sides. Right close by them was another prayer area with saints and angels. It had small streams with flowers. It was like a perfect garden. So rich in colors, so plush!

Again they took some time for prayer and praise. They spent some time just sitting and reflecting on everything about heaven.

Soon Angel Jennifer said, "We should be going. We are going to fly to another place here, yet!"

Soon they were above the trees in flight and they enjoyed the beautiful sides of the valley floor.

Wee Angel said, "There are streams, and waterfalls everywhere."

They flew and enjoyed the beauty of this valley.

Soon they flew up to a tall waterfall in the mountain. They flew to the topside with its vines of flowers. Again they walked along a stream, looked at all the flowers such as dahlia's, roses, rhododendrons, clematis vines, morning glories, and many more. It was so pretty!

Then ahead of them, along the stream were great glories of light.

Angel Jennifer said, "It's another gateway, so we are going back to the gateway where we left our friends."

Soon they were through the gateway and in the light, with the thoughts and tears of this special quiet valley of prayer. It was so serenely majestic. It stirred their hearts and heavenly soul, again the joy of heaven.

Chapter 11

Spending Time with Friends

They flew back in the light. After they had flown in heaven's time they came back through the beautiful, golden archway that the Creator had made for everyone. Soon they landed and they walked on a little until they saw their friends.

Noah, Annie, and Golden all were quietly lying on heaven's rich carpet of grass by some trees.

Angel Gabriella said, "It's so good to see them."

Felicia flew up on Starbright's back. Angel Daniella and Angel Gabriella were getting little flowers and putting them in each one's hair.

Angel Daniella said, "They are so wonderful, Felicia and Wee Angel. I'm so thankful to know you and them."

Angel Gabriella had some tears. "Love is very powerful and heaven has so much love of one another."

Soon Angel Jennifer said, "I have to be going!"

Soon after hugs, she flew along the golden path to another area.

Angel Gabriella and Angel Daniella said the same that they had to be at another place in heaven. So they too, gave hugs, more hugs and soon both said, "Wee Angel, Felicia, we will see you again! We will find you."

So off they flew along the path in the same direction as Angel Jennifer had flown.

Felicia and Wee Angel were soon on Starbright's back. They decided to leave Annie, Golden, Majestic and Noah there. So more hugs to each and they spent some time playing and running with each one, but soon knew they were to go on to another place in heaven.

Soon they were on the back of Starbright and he flew over more of heaven's land. They came to a large stream or smaller river so Wee Angel had Starbright fly along this just above the trees and heavenly lands.

There were other winged horses with passengers in flight along it's edges. "Wee Angel," Felicia said, "I'm having such a blessed time with all the friends, saints, and angels we have met here."

Soon they neared a forest of trees that had brooks flowing around and through them with short stepped waterfalls, many flowers at their edges. Along side the stream was an open grazing area so Starbright landed there.

Wee Angel said, "We need to nap some and the rest never hurts Starbright." Both with cushion-like flowers under them had a wonderful, heavenly nap. Several saints walked close by them. Wee Angel and Felicia talked with Christine, Josh, Kathy, Katie, Anthony, and Ken.

They also prayed and talked about everything that they had seen in heaven.

Josh said, "Thank you Lord and be with them in their journey. We are so blessed to have met them. We pray that we can fellowship and meet them again. Thank you, Lord. We love you, Jesus and Lord God. Thank you from all of us here. Amen!"

"That was so nice of you, Josh." said Wee Angel. All of the younger saints were just a little bigger than our Wee Angel.

All of them bid each other good-days and soon they walked along the golden path as there were horses in the area for the saints and angels.

Wee Angel said, "It's been wonderful."

It was so peaceful with each having a lot of love and joy, this joy of heaven!

Chapter 12

Jesus and many Winged Horses with Riders

As they stood on the open grass, they enjoyed their surroundings. They enjoyed the heavenly way.

Wee Angel looked and said, "Look, Felicia, some winged horses with riders are coming closer to us."

She continued, "It is the winged horses and power riders. See all the power of light about them."

In the distance, these horses and riders were getting closer to them. They were not flying that fast, just getting closer and closer to them.

"What a sight!" said Felicia, jumping up and down with excitement.

Soon they were close enough to know it was Jesus on Revelation (Sir William). He had over a hundred riders on horses with him.

Both Wee Angel and Felicia were counting as best they could the number, as they slowly landed by them on the grass open area.

Both agreed as Wee Angel said, "There are around 150 winged horses with riders, Felicia."

They were still landing in a very orderly way, so it was such a majestic sight to see as these riders land their horses.

Jesus on Revelation had touched unto heaven's land.

Felicia and Wee Angel knelt as Jesus walked closer to them with Revelation. Jesus said, "I think you two, have a friend here you want to see!"

With that Felicia and Wee Angel ran to give a big hug to Revelation who was always excited to see them.

All the riders stood besides their white winged horses at attention as Jesus talked with Wee Angel and Felicia. Behind two of the riders were some friends of Felicia's and Wee Angel.

Felicia said to Jesus, "It's Angel Gabriella and Angel Daniella!"

Jesus added, "Yes, my children! We were grazing the horses when they flew up to us and I asked them to join us. Angel Gabriella said they had been with you so we decided to have all of you join us for a nice ride. How's that?"

"Really, Jesus!" said Felicia.

"Yes, really!" smiled Jesus.

With this Jesus motioned towards the leader of the riders, and said, "We have four special riders going with us!"

Now approaching them were two of the riders.

Soon Jesus said, "Felicia, this is David and Joshua. I'm sure you have heard of them from my Word."

Felicia's eyes were as wide as they could get as she put her hands up to her face and kept saying, "Oh my! Oh My!"

She was so excited and kept saying, "Oh my, Oh my!"

She ran and hugged both of them. David lifted Felicia up and gave her the biggest hug. Joshua was giving Wee Angel a big hug.

Joshua said, "I've heard a lot about you. Wee Angel has been taking good care of you!"

After this Felicia said, "Can I give you a hug, Jesus?"

"Yes, now it is alright," as Jesus picked up Felicia and gave her a big hug. "My little one! You are in your home now!"

Angel Gabriella and Angel Daniella were there and both had to have hugs too! David and Joshua looked so handsome and strong. With Jesus the radiance of his face was so awesome. Again they had on riding attire!

The scene was serene, yet so powerfully beautiful!

With this, Jesus took heavenly time, and led them in prayer. Wee Angel, Felicia, Angel Gabriella, and Angel Daniella listened to every word Jesus prayed, and again more tears filled their eyes. It seemed like they could not stop the flowing of the tears.

When Jesus finished his prayer, he picked each one up again, hugged them and said, "Just know I love each one of you very much! I now have to talk to David and Joshua."

Out of the tears, all four said to Jesus, "We are so thankful to know you. We love you so much!"

Jesus had a tear in his eye. Quietly, he smiled, turned, walked with David and Joshua to the leader of the riders.

They talked and again the riders and the white winged horses rested on heaven's lands.

Angels gathered to the sides of them in the heavenly skies, up and around them. They continued to gather away in the glories of heaven.

Wee Angel said to Felicia, "They always start to gather, wherever Jesus is!"
Felicia, Wee Angel, Angel Gabriella, and Angel Daniella were grooming Revelation and gave him attention. He loved every minute of it.

Jesus took David, Joshua, and the leader of the riders to the side where they talked. Wee Angel and Felicia could tell by the conversation that it was very important. The discussion went on for quite some time, even heavenly time.

Then in heavenly time, Joshua came over to them and said Jesus wants you to come with us as we go for a special ride.

Felicia had again some tears of joy on her cheeks. They just kept flowing, and pretty soon, Wee Angel had some tears too!

Even Joshua was so humbled by them. All of them humbled by everything. Angel Gabriella said, "I'm so glad you have us with, Wee Angel and Felicia." "Thank you again," said Angel Daniella.

The heavenly moment was very SPECIAL. Jesus was special. Joshua, David and the leader of the riders were special. It was so humbling to hear Jesus pray, as their little hearts with filled with joy. This joy of heaven. It's that way in heaven!

Daniel Leske

Chapter 13

Jesus, David, Joshua, Leader and Conference

The angels continued to gather quietly above everyone and the white winged horses. They hovered above, quietly and the whole scene was so majestically awesome. Felicia noticed and commented on this.

Angel Daniella said, "They always do this for Jesus. Now they are ultra quiet. They are so very quiet."

All four of them had wonderment on their minds because of this. They knew something was to unfold, because of the conversation by Jesus, David, Joshua, and the leader of the riders. They also knew this because the angels were so quiet in the heavenly sky.

Then after quite some heaven's time, a signal was given and they were ready to go!

Angel Gabriella had gotten a purple orchid and placed it on the mane of Revelation.

Then David walked over to them and said, "Felicia, you will ride behind me. Wee Angel, you will ride behind Joshua. Angel Daniella and Angel Gabriella, you will ride behind the two riders you came with to get here. Starbright will be flying with us too, as we will have an extra rider for him. He has flown with us many times, as he again is a very special, powerful winged horse."

Starbright stood out from the other white winged horses.

"Thank you." said Felicia.

That's all it took as she showed her heavenly emotions.

The white winged horses looked so powerful as the whole area had so much power and energy. They looked majestic, perfect in everything.

The riders again had on light colored attire with gems of light from their shoulders. Beams of light went out and away from them. The horses with bridles and saddles again were awesomely beautiful and refined in appearance as they stood there.

First Jesus on Revelation and then the other riders on these beautiful white winged horses were ready for flight.

In an orderly fashion, Jesus on Revelation was soon in flight as the other horses followed him.

Soon, they were in flight above heaven's land. Felicia sat behind David and loved every moment. She waved, of course, to Wee Angel, Angel Daniella and Angel Gabriella. Once in the heavenly sky, each winged horse and rider spaced themselves perfectly in formation to the sides with Jesus on Revelation in front. As they flew along, Felicia felt the tremendous power that was present around them. Glories of power surrounded the riders and horses. It was not the same as when Felicia and Wee Angel had ridden on Sir William.

"As Revelation, he is so powerful!" Felicia said to David.

He nodded in agreement and said, "My child, you are right!"

They flew, not too fast, but onward. They now flew higher than most saints. Rolling hills, rivers, and golden paths passed under these riders. What a magnificent sight as other saints watched them.

They knew it was Jesus, knelt if close as they saw Jesus with the riders pass over them.

Onward, they flew, glories of light coming from them, going in all directions. Angel Gabriella, Angel Daniella, Wee Angel and Felicia had the biggest smiles on their faces. They were so happy as they sat behind the two riders, Joshua, and David.

On they flew, Jesus and his riders. All apart of this joy of heaven.

Chapter 14

A Quiet Ride Starts

They flew onward across heaven's lands, so majestic, so beautiful so peaceful! These powerful, beautiful white winged horses and riders. They journeyed over meadows, saints, along rivers and streams. A mighty sight, it was, with this tremendous formation of horses and riders. Onward they flew in formation. Their flight was as beautiful as it could be across these heaven's lands.

Felicia and Wee Angel waved to each other again from their horses. The horses had power and might!

Then as they flew, they noticed more glories of light starting to form to their sides. Wee Angel, Felicia had seen this when they entered the archways for flight, yet there was something different, for they sensed a lot of power about and all around the horses as a unit.

David quietly said, "Felicia, be prepared, for something very special that is going to happen! Jesus talked to Joshua, the leader and I when we stood on heaven's land. Just hang on as we ride and know that this is all for a reason." Felicia said, "Thank you, David."

He went on, "Joshua will let Wee Angel know and the riders will let Angel Gabriella and Angel Daniella know about this."

The light and power was growing brighter and brighter.

Glories from them now flowed all across heaven's land. It glowed with intensity, if seen close by, or at a distance. On they flew, and flew, and flew! They flew steadily onward!
Then after a lengthy time in flight, they flew faster and faster! All to their sides

was light and more light. Power and more power!

Then, clouds started to build in front of these flying horses. Clouds of power and light as they flew they were flying upward like through the archways, but clouds kept forming in front, to the front, to the sides, and below them, and above them as these winged horses flew onward!

It was so majestically beautiful.

Felicia said, "I feel so much power about us. David, thank you again for taking us with you."

"It's alright, our child! We are happy to have you!" answered David.
Meanwhile Wee Angel was talking with Joshua.

Angel Gabriella and Angel Daniella were very quietly talking to the riders.
Jesus on Revelation was in the very front of the formation of white winged horses as they flew along, as his glories were always more brighter than the others.

There was glorious light, radiant colors, golden hues, and aquas, of strong radiance about him as he rode on this beautiful white winged horse called Revelation. How majestic the scene was with clouds of power and might about these horses. They flew upward and onward.

Soon ahead a huge valley formed of clouds and power! As they flew along, in time, as far as they could see ahead was this huge valley made by clouds. The clouds were forming way, way, way ahead of the unit of winged horses and riders.

More and more the clouds kept forming the valley, kept building up, making a path to follow for the riders on these beautiful white winged horses.

Then more groups of white winged horses were in front and to the sides of Jesus group. A huge group of white winged horses with riders was far left of Jesus group. A huge group of white winged horses to the far right and ahead as Jesus group approached them. A leader was in front of each group.
David said, "They are a part of the Lord's army! Just know that! This is talked

about in the Bible. This is part of Lord God Almighty's heavenly army."

David went on, "The leader to the left is Moses. The leader to the right is Abraham. They are strong in stature like their younger days on earth."

Felicia said, "They look like warriors of Christ now."

"Yes, they do!" answered David.

Abraham and Moses had their groupings of riders on winged horses follow up and behind the riders of Jesus. These units had many more white winged horses than the unit with Jesus. The whole formation became much longer and wider, as they flew along, while the glories of the power surrounding everyone was increasing mightily!

Daniel Leske

Chapter 15

A Mighty Mission

As they flew along, there were walls of clouds to both sides of them, with the unit in flight flying between these high walls of clouds. High above them tremendous glories of light across to the tops of the clouds. Way below the riders on winged horses clouds formations were forming and had already formed as they flew in between all of the clouds.

Then as they flew up ahead and in an opening of the wall of clouds was another grouping of riders and winged horses to their left and to their right. The new groups were in flight, headed closer to the Lord's unit.

They were coming through openings in this huge valley of clouds.

David explained, "The leader of the riders to the left is Samuel! The leader of the horses to the right is Simon Peter.."

When Felicia heard his name, she had a tear quickly form in her eye.
"Simon Peter," she kept saying, "Simon Peter! Simon Peter!"

She continued, "How inside, so many of us cried on earth over his ups and downs. He is so special in a different way."

"Child," David said, "He is to Jesus and us too! Still is!"

The units with Samuel and Simon Peter leading flew in behind the main unit. Jesus was still out front of all these riders on white winged horses.

As they continued to fly onward, angels were gathering more and more along and above on the valley of the cloud's walls. They were quietly flying in and hovering all along the clouds, thousands of angels from other places in heaven. More and more angels were gathering to the sides, to the front and in front on the walls formed by the clouds.

Jesus with the white winged horses continued to fly onward.

The angels were more and more to the sides of them now, from far below to high above. All along the sides, the angels were quickly flying in and they were quiet as they hovered in the beautiful glories along the clouds.

The moment was quiet in heaven. Glories all over, but heaven was very quiet and serene as something was coming ahead of Jesus riding with his riders.

Felicia said to David, "I can't believe what I am seeing!"

All the angels, hovered, while more and more appeared or flew in along the sides by the clouds. They still were very quiet!

David said, "There is a reason!"

The white winged horses including Revelation and the many, many riders flew onward, and after heavenly time in flight, David and Felicia started to hear the sounds of tremendous praise with glories to King Jesus.

All the riders on these beautiful horses started to hear praises coming from the direction ahead of them.

Before, the flight had been quiet, but now they heard sounds as they flew closer to these sounds of praise.

Then way up the valley in front of them was awesome light and light to the valleys sides. The valley of clouds was still to their sides and under them as Jesus continued to lead this army of winged horses and riders. Upward, to the sides, was much more light.

Revelation with Jesus was still way out in front of the riders and horses, while the sounds of praises were getting louder and louder.

Chapter 16

Jesus, Praises, Mission Continues

Felicia saw way out ahead a very vast open area that the valley of clouds was leading into it, where the valley had gotten much wider. Before the huge open area of the valley, Archangel Michael with Archangel Raphael were standing in tremendous light to the left and Archangel Gabriel with Archangel Micah were standing in tremendous light to the right. Other archangels stood along side of them.

They could hear more and more the sounds of praises being sung and spoken by the angels that in this vast open area where the valley of clouds.

Jesus, leading this huge formation of white winged horses, flew onward slowly getting, closer and closer to this huge open valley with the all the praises.

"Praise the Father! Praises to our Lord," the voices were shouting!

"My the praises we are hearing!" Felicia spoke to David.

The formation of horses flew closer and closer to the sounds of praise! Revelation flew onward!

Ahead of them where the valley of clouds opened and widened, angels were up and away to the sides. Thousands and thousands of angels praised the Lord.

Jesus with the army of white winged horses and riders flew closer. The praises got louder and louder! Wee Angel quietly glanced at Felicia as both David and Joshua flew fairly close together in the formation. Wee Angel smiled, yet in her eyes, she had a few tears. Felicia had some too! They never expected anything like this to happen!

"Jesus," they heard on their horses. "Jesus! Jesus!"

Over and over they shouted "Jesus!"

The horses and riders flew even closer to the widened valley of all angels to the sides. They neared the archangels.

The archangels then flew to the outside of the winged horses and riders as the formation was now drawing closer to the vast wide valley of thousands, and thousands, of angels in praise.

"Jesus... Jesus... Jesus," the riders kept hearing.

Then soon this mighty formation of white horses, riders with Jesus in the very front flew into this wide, wide open area with thousands and thousands and thousands of angels along the sides by the clouds. A vast very wide-like room in the valley of the clouds.

A cheer went up of glories and praise as the riders flew into this widened valley. The sounds were now loud and awesome!

Then they broke out in tremendous praise shouting, "Hallelujah to the King! Hallelujah to Jesus our King! Hallelujah to the Father! Hallelujah to Jesus!"

Onward they flew thru and in the valley of angels in mighty praise!

They flew onward, onward and onward!

The sounds of praise never ceased! The angels continued to shout and shout and shout!

At times many angels would blow trumpets, a mighty powerful sound!

The shouts continued as the angels shouted, "Jesus... Jesus... Jesus!"
Felicia, Wee Angel's, Angel Gabriella's and Angel Daniella's eyes were so very

wide open because of all the intensity around them. They held to the one that was in control of the horse.

The white winged horses flew onward, onward, and onward!

It was glories of light, all around, yet angels to their sides and below them were clouds. They kept flying through this wide valley of clouds and angels.

As they flew it was all angels to their sides as well as ahead of them, as far as they could see!

Above them, the angels hovered up into the glories of light. They had been flying a long time with thousands of angels.

Onward they flew!

"Jesus!"

Onward they flew!

"Jesus!"

Onward they flew

"Jesus!"

The shouts continued, "Jesus… Jesus… Jesus!"

The shouts rang through the heavens.

In the front of this mighty formation of many, many winged white horses, Jesus led the riders as they flew onward. The archangels continued to fly by the sides of these mighty heavenly power riders and their horses. They were on a mission!

Chapter 17

Paul, Solomon, The Army Grows

Jesus with the white winged horses flew onward. Ahead of them, to the left, to the right, again were some open spaces in the valley of clouds along the sides. To the left, was another of white winged horse units and to the right another white winged horse unit. They were slowly flying towards the main formation of horses.

David said to Felicia, "Paul is leading his unit from the left and Solomon is leading his unit from the right."

As the main formation of winged horses flew onward with Jesus leading everyone, they flew slowly in behind the main formation and took their place in flight along with the rest.

Onward they flew in this wide valley of clouds!

Angels, up and along the sides shouting, "Jesus... Jesus... Jesus... Jesus"

Onward they flew!

"Jesus!"

Onward they flew!

"Jesus!"

Onward they flew!

"Jesus!"

Onward they flew, as more shouts, "Jesus our King! Lord of All! Jesus Our King!"

"Praise to the Father!"

"Praise to our King!"

Onward they flew!

"Jesus!"

Onward they flew!"

"Jesus!"

Onward they flew!

"Jesus!"

Praises continued as the mighty formation of horses flew onward, as the thousands of angels continued to praise the Lord.

Jesus on Revelation flew onward!

The army of heaven flew onward!

The archangels flew onward!

"Jesus!"

Then after heaven's time, there were less and less angels along the sides of the valley of clouds. The valley had also narrowed further or was like it was earlier in their flight. Slowly there were less and less angels. Then very few angels along the sides, just the many clouds that made up the valley.

Onward the formation flew and Felicia said to David, "Look way up in front of us. I can see the clouds stirring and forming this valley."

David nodded in agreement, "Look closer."

Felicia saw tremendous light energy, causing these clouds to form. They saw this tremendous energy of light rolling and pushing! They saw tremendous fires of light!

This mighty formation of white winged horses flew straight onward, staying within the valley, and headed towards this tremendous light.

Way ahead of them, as they flew, they could see the light pushing darkness of space out and away, with the clouds forming right behind this tremendous fires and light. This was a long distance ahead of the riders in flight.

Felicia held David tighter! Light continued to push away darkness to the sides way ahead of them, with the clouds forming right behind, yet ahead of the riders. Then way ahead she saw the darkness of the universe and ahead and in the darkness was a planet as the white winged horses with these riders in flight headed straight towards this planet. Revelation flew onward!

Felicia said to David, "What is it? We seem to be flying straight towards it."

David said, "I'm afraid, you are familiar with this place. It's EARTH! We are headed towards it."

Angels followed this massive unit of winged horses and riders. Archangels were flying along side of the formation. The earth was their destination as valley of clouds continued to form and the extremely power light, rolling, streaming with fires which formed the valley as it pushed the darkness.

The mighty formation with Jesus continued to fly onward! The Archangels flew onward! The angels were flying along the sides as well! Everyone was quiet, except there were mighty sounds that came from the light and forces of it.

They could see earth was getting bigger and bigger.

Onward they flew! Onward they flew! Closer and closer to earth. Earth was getting bigger and bigger ahead of them as this tremendous formation of power and riders was headed straight to earth. All the riders were in the Army of Heaven as spoken about in Revelation 19:14.

Then it HAPPENED! Jesus who was leading, turned his head to the leader of all the riders. With one stroke of his right arm, he signaled the leader to turn and head back.

At the same time Jesus raised his right arm, up and about in the same motion, an extremely large right arm and hand signaled in the same manner. It was the arm of Lord God Almighty made of light and fire.

In a loud commanding voice that ripped through to all the riders, archangels, and angels, Jesus, together, at the same time, with Lord God Almighty, spoke, "It is not quite time yet, but be ready!"

Slowly Jesus with all the riders slowly headed their horses in a large turn and slowly turned, flew, headed back to heaven through the valley of clouds and light. Back to their homeland for the time is not quite yet!

Everyone knew in their hearts that this right arm of God's would be right with the heavenly army when this mission would happen to earth.

They flew, and flew, and flew!

Angels were still in the valley along the way, praised Jesus, and kept praising as the riders on these horses flew back and on! They kept flying back through the clouds and valley of angels that had gathered there.

David said to Felicia, "You are a part of this, more than you will ever know! The Father, Son, and the Holy Spirit, said it is not quite time. When we go to earth, we will be ready for it!"

Felicia said, "I know what you mean!"

Joshua said the same to Wee Angel as they talked about it too!

Jesus was very quiet. Jesus riding on Revelation continued to fly in front with all the power about them. He was quiet the whole time as this happened.

Felicia said to David, "I wonder what Jesus is thinking?"

David said, "He doesn't say much about this, but all sense it weighs heavily on him."

They flew onward, back to heaven's land. Within heaven's time, they were all back in all the glories of light. This special place called heaven. As Felicia said, "It's now my home."

Daniel Leske

Chapter 18

Heaven's Land after a Mission

Within heaven's time, they flew more away from the clouds of glory, and the angels that had gathered, back to heaven's lands that were ahead of them as they quietly flew onward.

Wee Angel and Felicia were very joyful over the experience, yet they were silent because of what the ride might have been about, if the ride headed to earth.

Paul with his riders and Solomon with his riders, on command from Jesus started to fly away from the main formation. Then Peter and Samuel led their riders away from the main formation. Then Abraham and then Moses led their riders. Soon it was Jesus, Joshua, and David with the leader and the rest of the riders.

David said, "We are headed to one of the gates to the Lord's City, and there is where we will land with the horses."

Onward they flew, now across some of heaven's lands. They could see some of the tremendous glories of God's City. Onward they flew with a mighty flight by Revelation as Jesus led the riders.

Felicia said to David, "How majestic he is in flight! I can't get over all the beautiful times Wee Angel and I have been on the back of Revelation!"

David said, "He is a beautiful heavenly animal! He is so special to Jesus and we love Revelation too!"

Revelation flew onward. Within time, they neared an open area, just outside of God's City. There were angels that hovered above the sides of the opening with golden roads that led away from and to the City.

Again the gate was different from the others that they had been through on their journeys.

It was like the sides of God's Holy Mountain were right by the gate. There were two very wide waterfalls along each side of the golden road into the city. Roses and hedges made everything look so beautiful. The falls were wide, and also there were small steps to the stream as it went out and around the outside of the mountain. Trees surrounded the open grass areas to the city. Hedges with flowers, and golden walkways.

Within time, all the white winged horses and riders with Jesus stood on the beautiful grass of heaven. Joshua and David talked with the leader of the riders while Wee Angel and Felicia waited by some flowers, then they signaled to Angel Gabriella and Angel Daniella to come to them.

Jesus said, "Thank you, my special ones. I know it wasn't the ride you expected! I know your were alright, totally protected and all of us were happy you came with us."

Angels hovered above, quietly and around the sides. Jesus said again to them, "I think there are some friends of yours over by the grouping of trees. They have been waiting there for you. I'm heading back into the city to be apart of the throne."

With that Jesus picked each one up and gave them a big hug! He knew the importance of the ride. He knew the love he had for others such as Wee angel, Felicia, Angel Gabriella, and Angel Daniella.

He sighed and said, "I'll see you again!"

With this, he quietly turned to David and Joshua and said, "Let's go!"

The little ones were on their knees with some tears in their eyes!

Jesus, David, and Joshua walked slowly on the golden way and headed into His Holy City. Then they turned and smiled, and David said, "Go see your friends now."

With this, Angel Gabriella, Felicia, Wee Angel and Angel Daniella got up and ran over to the wooded area.

Meanwhile Jesus, David and Joshua walked between the two wide waterfalls and through another beautiful gate with glories, and soft light. Angels hovered and sang praises as at the other gates. They walked on into God's Holy City.

Daniel Leske

Chapter 19

Revelation, Starbright and Tuddley and Friends

The leader of the riders had been holding Revelation. Then he said, "Go Revelation, go to the children!" He walked and then ran to the woods to see everyone.

All of them again gave hugs to each other. There was Tuddley Teddy, Annie, Majestic, Noah, Toby and Golden.

All of them got many hugs and Revelation was warmly welcomed by all of them. It was amazing how strong Revelation seemed after such a long flight. These winged horses have awesome strength.

They were all joyful with their little friends. Angel Daniella and Angel Gabriella, then flew and put flowers in each one. They made sure that Starbright had a special flower too, and a nice big hug. They had grown to like him like their other animal friends. Starbright stood beside Revelation as they rested from the long flight.

All of them were a little quiet because of the long ride that they had been on with the riders. Yet now, they were back on heaven's lands with their friends.

Angel Gabriella said to them, "Let's all form a circle and have some prayer."

The four with the animals close to them held hands in a circle prayer!

Angel Gabriella led the prayer, "Dear Lord, We pray for those on earth. We pray that they come to know you and how beautiful you are in everything! You are the Creator, thank you for my friends and animal friends. We love you!"

Angel Daniella said, "Yes, we love you, Lord!"

Wee Angel said, "Yes, Father, we love you! "Felicia said, "Jesus, I love you. We love you and we thank you!"

All said "Amen."

They sat under the trees and talked, and talked while the animals laid beside them. Angels still hovered above the grass. It was heavenly quiet. They also were very tired, so they slept under the trees with their friends. It was good for all of them, including Revelation. So they did rest, as it was a serene moment, and quiet because of the ride.

In heaven's time, they awoke, they had so much on their hearts, not only for Jesus and heaven, but a burden about earth. They had wonderment as to its destination and what they knew from the scriptures. Also the decision, the Father had to make over this. They knew, and yet they didn't know about the time.

Felicia said, "I'm so overwhelmed with everything. I've been a part of so much love."

Wee Angel agreed, as did the two identical twin angels. Soon after reflecting the moment, they got up and hugged all their little friends, and the biggest hug for Revelation. He nodded his head. He looked like he was going to horse cry. This love! This joy!

The four were together again with their friends.

Felicia said, "We love you all so much!"

Angel Gabriella, Angel Daniella, Wee Angel and Felicia laughed, smiled! The animals wiggled all over with all the joy in their hearts.

They all looked at God's City and thought again of Jesus. They again thought of joy! They flew up and around their friends; they again felt a need to hug all their little friends. Love was strong, in this moment, with all the thoughts, on their hearts.

Then they decided to pray again, and each one said, "Thank you, Jesus, that heaven is our home."

With this, Toby, Tuddley Teddy, Annie, Noah with Majestic on his back, and Golden walked up to Angel Daniella, Angel Gabiella, Felicia, and Wee Angel. They were ready to see more of heaven.

Daniel Leske is available for speaking engagements and public appearances. For more information contact:

Daniel Leske
C/O Advantage Books
P.O. Box 160847
Altamonte Springs, FL 32716

info@ advbooks.com

Daniel has also published *The Joy of Heaven 1, The Joy of Heaven 2* and *The Joy of Heaven 3*, all available from *Advantage Books*

To purchase additional copies of this book or other books published by *Advantage Books* call our order number at:

407-788-3110 (Book Orders Only)

or visit our bookstore website at: www.advbookstore.com

We are planning to have some children's products of the characters from *The Joy of Heaven 1, 2, 3 and 4*. They would be stuffed animal toys, teddy bears, figurines, possibly dolls and other products. For more information:

www.thejoyofheaven.com

Facebook: Daniel Leske / Author

*A*dvantage
BOOKS

Longwood, Florida, USA
"we bring dreams to life"™
www.advbookstore.com

www.ingramcontent.com/pod-product-compliance
Lightning Source LLC
Chambersburg PA
CBHW081520040426

42447CB00013B/3283

9 781597 554084